ALASKA

U.S.A. TRAVEL GUIDES

BY ANN HEINRICHS • ILLUSTRATED BY MATT KANIA

The Child's World®
childsworld.com

Published by The Child's World®
1980 Lookout Drive • Mankato, MN 56003-1705
800-599-READ • www.childsworld.com

Photo Credits
Photographs ©: Mike Redwine/Shutterstock Images,
cover, 1; Scott McMurren CC2.0, 7; Mark Byzewski
CC2.0, 8; Emma Forsberg CC2.0, 11; John Pennell/U.S.
Army Alaska (USARAK), 12; Library of Congress, 13;
iStockphoto, 15; National Park Service, 16, 27; Joshua
Strang/U. S. Air Force, 19; LaRoche/Library of Congress,
20; North Wind Picture Archives, 21; Al Grillo/AP Images,
23; U.S. Geological Survey, 24; Carol M. Highsmith/
Carol M. Highsmith's America Project in the Carol M.
Highsmith Archive/Library of Congress, 28; Katrina
Outland/Shutterstock Images, 31; Eric Engman/Fairbanks
Daily News-Miner/AP Images, 32; Shutterstock Images,
35, 37

ISBN 9781503819429
LCCN 2016961118

Printing
Printed in the United States of America
PA02334

post card

About the Author
Ann Heinrichs

Ann Heinrichs is the author
of more than 100 books
for children and young
adults. She has also enjoyed
successful careers as a
children's book editor and
an advertising copywriter.
Ann grew up in Fort Smith,
Arkansas, and lives in
Chicago, Illinois.

post card

About the
Map Illustrator
Matt Kania

Matt Kania loves maps and, as a
kid, dreamed of making them. In
school he studied geography and
cartography, and today he makes
maps for a living. Matt's favorite
thing about drawing maps is
learning about the places they
represent. Many of the maps
he has created can be found in
books, magazines, videos, Web
sites, and public places.

On the cover: Mendenhall Glacier near Juneau
is surrounded by meadows and mountains.

OUR ALASKA TRIP

Ready to explore the Last **Frontier**? Just hop aboard. We're heading north to Alaska! You'll meet sled dogs and polar bears. You'll see the sun shine at midnight. You'll see glaciers and stroll among totem poles. You'll fish for halibut and pan for gold. Can you dig it? Then buckle up and hang on tight. We're off!

WELCOME TO
ALASKA

ARCTIC OCEAN

RUSSIA

Who Lived Here before Europeans Arrived? Aleut, Athabaskan, Haida, Inuit, Tlingit, and Tsimshian

The ancestors of Alaska's Native Americans probably came from Asia. Alaska and Russia were once connected by land. That would be a long trip!

CANADA

Anchorage

PACIFIC OCEAN

Today, there are 11 groups of Alaska Natives. They speak 20 different languages.

THE ALASKA NATIVE HERITAGE CENTER IN ANCHORAGE

You're hearing ancient stories. You're holding tools made of moose **antlers**. People are dancing in beaded hides. You're at the Alaska Native Heritage Center in Anchorage!

Here you'll learn all about Alaska's Natives. They began living in Alaska thousands of years ago. They hunted and fished. They made their own clothes, tools, and houses. Some made homes with whale bones. Some made lamps that burned seal oil. Everyone took what they needed from their surroundings.

More than five million Native Americans live in Alaska today. They make up approximately two percent of Alaska's population. They continue to preserve their heritage by keeping their tribal **traditions** alive.

Watch Native Alaskan dancers perform at the Alaska Native Heritage Center.

Y ou are in a forested area. You look up and see a painted wooden pole. A **thunderbird** with outstretched wings is at the top. Other animals have been carved below the thunderbird. One looks like a fox. Another looks like a bear.

You are strolling through Saxman Totem Park in Ketchikan. These works of art are totem poles. Alaska's Tlingit and Haida people carved these poles. Each animal belongs to a family unit, or clan. The totem poles tell **legends** or histories about that clan. The animals are also the guardians of the household.

Approximately one in six Alaskans is a Native. Many still hunt and fish for a living. They also carry on their arts and customs. One of these important customs is the carving of totem poles.

Each totem pole at Saxman Totem Park tells a story.

8

Each animal means something! Ravens are tricky, frogs bring wealth, and wolves make friends with ghosts.

Only Wyoming and Vermont have fewer people than Alaska.

ARCTIC OCEAN

RUSSIA

In 2016, 741,894 people lived in Alaska. It's the 48th-largest state by population.

Fairbanks •

Anchorage •

CANADA

Juneau ★

PACIFIC OCEAN

Ketchikan •

Total Population of Largest Communities
Anchorage.................298,695
Juneau..........................32,756
Fairbanks.....................32,325

There are 25 totem poles at Saxman Totem Park.

THE ANCHORAGE FUR RENDEZVOUS

Is she flying? Is she falling from the sky? Not quite! It's the Anchorage Fur **Rendezvous**. And you're watching Fur Rondy's blanket toss!

The Anchorage Fur Rendezvous is a three-day winter festival. It celebrates Alaska's fur trading history. Fur Rondy's blanket toss honors an Eskimo tradition. Eskimos celebrated whale hunts with a blanket toss. They held the edges of a big blanket. Then they tossed someone up in the air. It was just like a trampoline!

Russians were the first non-Natives in Alaska. They were explorers and fur traders. Traders and Native Americans would meet at a rendezvous. They shared food, customs, and news. And they played games such as the blanket toss!

See how high you can fly at Fur Rondy's blanket toss!

ALASKA DAY IN SITKA

Down comes the Russian flag. Up goes the American flag. It's Alaska Day in Sitka!

This festival celebrates a big day for Alaska. It was October 18, 1867. The place was Sitka, Alaska's Russian capital. That day, Russia transferred Alaska to the United States. People act out the ceremony every year. It happens on Sitka's Castle Hill.

William Seward was the U.S. secretary of state. He wanted to buy Alaska. People thought he was crazy. But Seward knew Alaska was a rich land. It had lots of fish, lumber, and minerals. How much did the United States pay for Alaska? More than $7 million!

Alaskans dressed as Russian sailors lower the Russian flag on Alaska Day.

ARCTIC OCEAN

RUSSIA

Dear Mr. Seward:
People laughed at you. They called your idea to buy Alaska "Seward's Icebox" and "Seward's **Folly**." But you got the last laugh! Alaska is a fantastic state!

Sincerely,
A Nature Lover

post card

Mr. William Seward
1801-1872
Washington, DC

The first Alaska Day was pretty messy. The Russian flag got tangled up. Someone had to climb up and cut it loose.

CANADA

PACIFIC OCEAN

Sitka •

Saint Michael's Cathedral in Sitka is a beautiful Russian Orthodox church.

Sitka was once a Tlingit village. Russians named it New Archangel.

Lowest Temperature: Prospect Creek near Stevens Village January 23, 1971 -80°F (-62°C)

Highest Temperature: Fort Yukon June 27, 1915 100°F (38°C)

Alaska is more than twice the size of Texas, the second-largest state.

ARCTIC OCEAN

Brooks Range

Arctic Region

CANADA

RUSSIA

Fort Yukon •

Stevens Village •

Why is Arctic tundra sometimes called a cold desert? Because it gets less rain than many deserts!

Alaska Range

Denali

Panhandle

Alaska Peninsula

Aleutian Islands

Alaska's western tip is only 51 miles (82 km) from Russia.

HIGHEST AND LOWEST POINTS
HIGHEST: Denali at 20,310 feet (6,190 m)
LOWEST: Sea level along the coast

Denali is a mountain in Alaska. It's in the Alaska Range. It's North America's highest peak.

Forty-eight U.S. states are connected to each other. Alaskans call them the Lower 48.

Smoosh. Squish. Squoosh. What's that under your feet? It's Arctic **tundra**!

Northern Alaska is in the Arctic Region. It faces the Arctic Ocean. Its icy soil is called tundra. This soil is frozen just beneath the surface. Tundra feels spongy to walk on.

Alaska is a big **peninsula**. Water surrounds almost all of it. Alaska has two long "tails." One is on the southeast. It's called the Panhandle. The other is on the southwest. It's the Alaska Peninsula and the Aleutian Islands.

Alaska has two big mountain ranges. The Brooks Range is in the north. In central Alaska is the Alaska Range. Alaska also has lots of glaciers. They look like mountains of ice.

Caribou live in Alaska's arctic tundra. Bears, moose, and wolves live there, too.

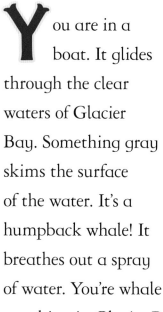

You are in a boat. It glides through the clear waters of Glacier Bay. Something gray skims the surface of the water. It's a humpback whale! It breathes out a spray of water. You're whale watching in Glacier Bay National Park.

Glacier Bay is near Juneau. It is surrounded by mountains. The mountain slopes are covered in snow and ice. These sheets of ice are called glaciers.

Glacier Bay is home to many animals. You might see eagles flying overhead. You might see seals or sea otters. You'd better bring a good camera! There are many things to see in Glacier Bay National Park.

Look for humpback whales in Glacier Bay. But try not to get splashed!

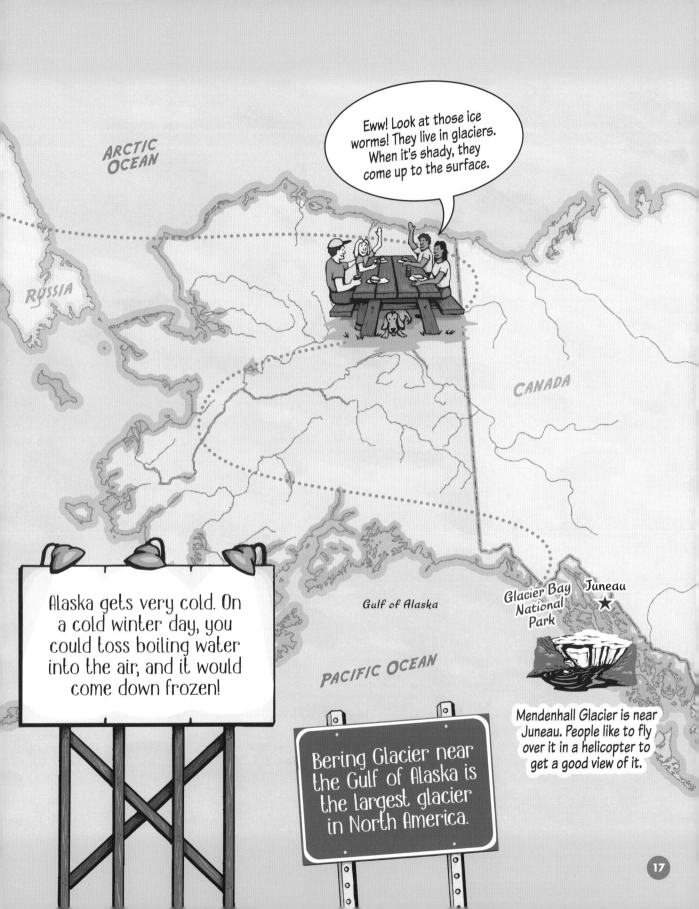

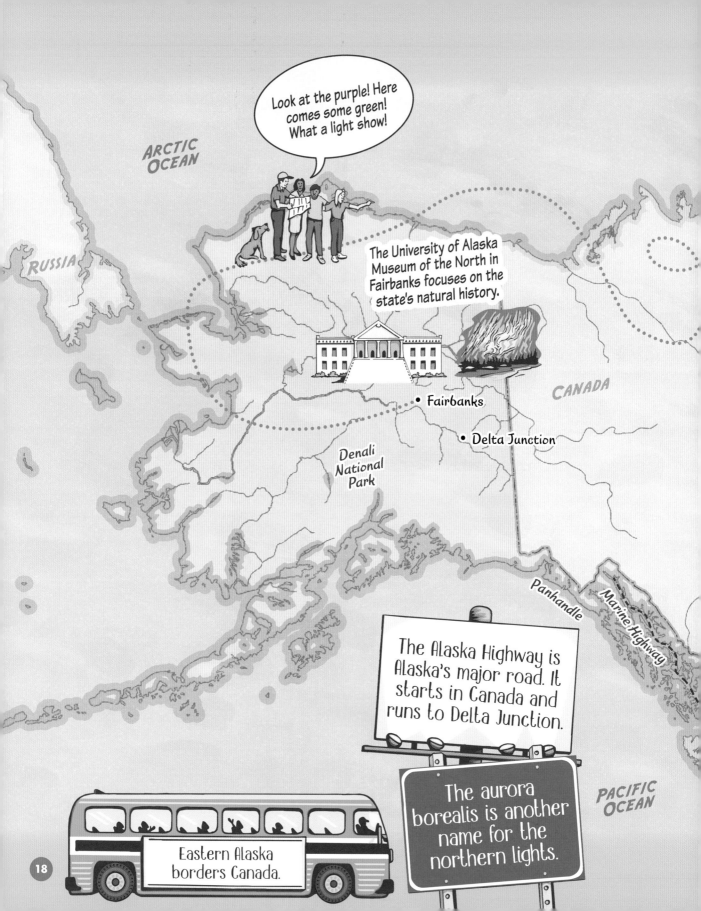

WATCHING THE NORTHERN LIGHTS

Go to Fairbanks, and wait for night to fall. You're in for a fantastic show! The northern lights are flashing across the sky. They're like dancing curtains of color! People come from miles away to see them.

There's a lot to do outdoors in Alaska. Some people like to watch the northern lights. Others climb mountains, ride kayaks, or fish. Denali National Park is popular, too. Park visitors can view wildlife or walk on a glacier.

There are many ways to get around in Alaska. Some people travel in bush planes. Others travel by train. The Marine Highway runs along the southeast coast. The southern part of the Marine Highway is called the Inside Passage. Many people cruise along this passage in boats. These boats are like water taxis!

The northern lights occur year-round but are most visible in winter.

LIARSVILLE AND THE KLONDIKE GOLD RUSH

There's a speck! There's a fleck! It's gold! You're panning for gold in Liarsville. It's just outside of Skagway.

Thousands of people swarmed into Skagway in 1897. They'd heard about gold in Canada's Klondike Region. The Klondike Region is in northwest Canada. One trail into the Klondike began in Skagway.

Liarsville stands where a gold-miner's camp used to be. According to legend, reporters camped there, too. They were looking for exciting stories to write. But they didn't want to hike to the Klondike. So they made up stories about big gold finds!

Klondike miners used horses and wagons to carry their supplies.

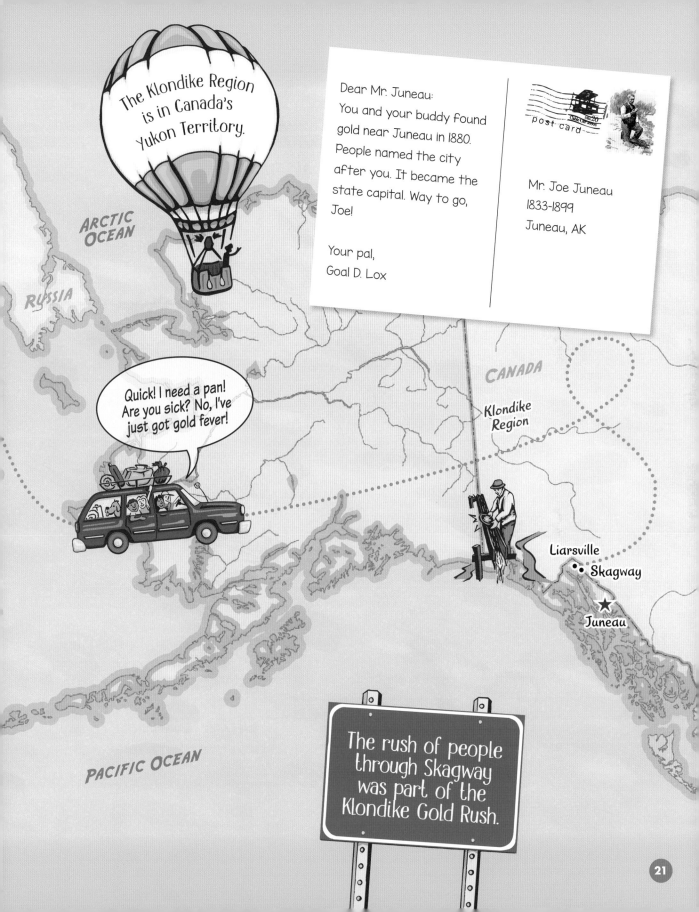

THE PRUDHOE BAY OIL FIELD

They work 12 hours a day. They sleep in **dorms**. They wear protective suits. This isn't a standard desk job. These people are working at Prudhoe Bay oil field.

Oil was discovered at Prudhoe Bay in 1968. It's way up on the north coast. Suddenly, oil became Alaska's richest product.

The oil at Prudhoe Bay is trapped underground. Workers drill down to reach it. Approximately 3,000 people work at Prudhoe Bay. Many work on the field for two weeks. Then they get two weeks off. Working at Prudhoe Bay oil field is no easy job!

Prudhoe Bay Oil Field workers inspect an oil pipeline.

THE TRANS-ALASKA PIPELINE

Holy moly! It's silvery and shiny. It's long and round and fat. And it's zigzagging across the tundra. Is it a monster snake? No, silly! It's just the Trans-Alaska Pipeline.

Oil mining is Alaska's biggest **industry**. Oil is the most valuable mining product, too. Most of the oil comes from Prudhoe Bay. The oil travels through that huge pipeline. It goes to the port of Valdez. That's along Alaska's southern coast. Look at that pipeline from the air. It looks like a big silver snake!

Moose, caribou, and other animals live on Alaska's tundra. There are more than 550 wildlife crossings built into the Trans-Alaska Pipeline. The pipeline is raised or buried beneath the ground in these places. This allows wildlife to cross through safely.

The Trans-Alaska Pipeline is hundreds of miles long. It passes through three mountain ranges.

KATMAI AND ITS FISHING BEARS

Swoosh! The bear scoops up a salmon. Chomp! What a great snack! This is no zoo. You're in Katmai National Park on the Alaska Peninsula. More than 2,000 brown bears live there. Can you guess their favorite food? Salmon!

Alaska has lots of bears, deer, and moose. Mountain goats and sheep live in the mountains. Polar bears roam along the icy north coast. You'll see seals and seabirds along the coast, too. Look out in the water. You might see whales leaping!

Not much grows on the northern tundra. Mostly there are mosses and short grasses. Caribou graze on these plants. Caribou are related to reindeer.

Bears work hard for their lunch! This brown bear has spotted a salmon in Katmai National Park.

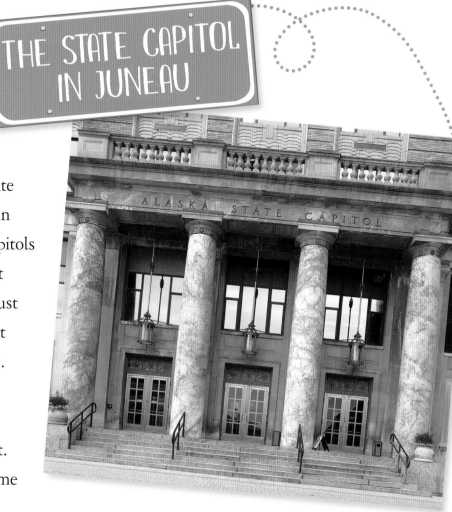

THE STATE CAPITOL IN JUNEAU

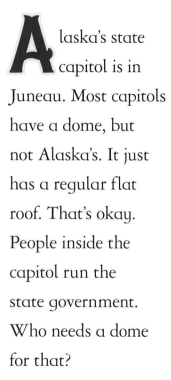

Alaska's state capitol is in Juneau. Most capitols have a dome, but not Alaska's. It just has a regular flat roof. That's okay. People inside the capitol run the state government. Who needs a dome for that?

Alaska has three branches of government. One branch makes the laws. It's called the legislature. Another branch carries out the laws. The governor heads this branch. The third branch consists of state courts. Their judges decide if laws have been broken.

The Alaska State Capitol was built in 1931.

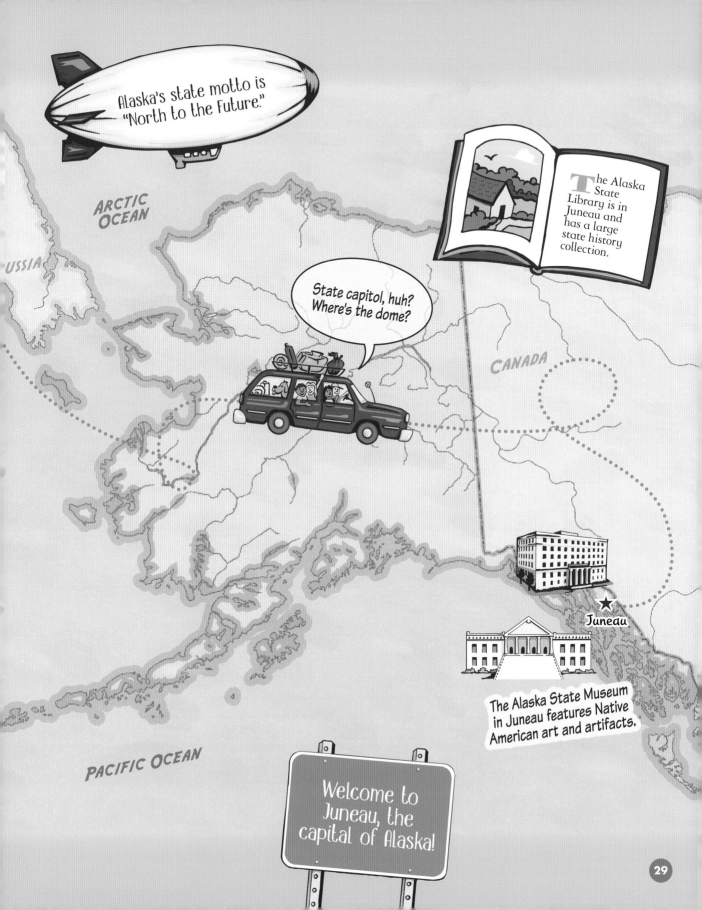

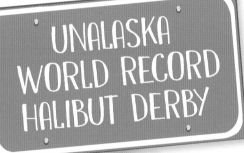

That is one big fish. But is it big enough? If it is, you get $1,000! You're at the Unalaska World Record Halibut Derby. Just catch the biggest halibut ever. Then you win the prize!

Alaska has the nation's biggest fishing industry. Unalaska is an important fishing port. It's in the Aleutian Islands. Kodiak is another important port. Crab, scallop, and shrimp are important catches. So are cod, flounder, and salmon. And don't forget that halibut!

Farming is a small industry in Alaska. The growing season is not very long. The short summer gets lots of sunshine, though. Some farming areas get 20 sunny hours a day!

Unalaska Island can only be reached by boat or plane.

BARROW AND THE MIDNIGHT SUN

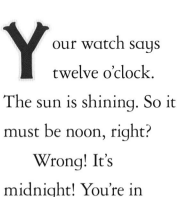

Your watch says twelve o'clock. The sun is shining. So it must be noon, right?

Wrong! It's midnight! You're in Barrow during the Midnight Sun!

Barrow is Alaska's most northerly city. Its summers are really sunny. The sun doesn't set for almost three months! It's the opposite in winter. For two whole months, the sun never rises!

How does the Midnight Sun happen? Like this. The Earth is tilted as it turns around. In the summer, the far north tilts toward the sun. That's why it gets more hours of sunshine. In the winter, the north is tilted the other way. It tilts away from the sun. Then the north gets more hours of darkness.

A crowd gathers for the Midnight Sun Baseball Game in Fairbanks.

32

The Iditarod is called the Last Great Race on Earth.

ARCTIC OCEAN

RUSSIA

Mush, you huskies! Mush!

• Nome

Mushers call directions to their dogs. "Gee!" means turn right. "Haw!" means turn left.

CANADA

• Anchorage

PACIFIC OCEAN

In 1985, Libby Riddles was the first woman to win the Iditarod. Susan Butcher won the race four times.

The Iditarod goes from Anchorage to Nome. That's almost 1,000 miles (1,600 km)!

Sled dogs wear booties to protect their feet.

NOME AND THE IDITAROD

The dogs dash to the finish line. Their tongues are hanging out. They've been racing for days and days. For those dogs, there's no place like Nome!

Nome is where the Iditarod ends. That's a sled dog race. The sled drivers are called mushers. Their dogs are huskies. They race over mountains, forests, and frozen rivers. They race through darkness, wind, and cold. At last, they can rest and eat some treats. Good doggies!

Each year, thousands of people travel to Alaska to see the Iditarod race.

OUR TRIP

We visited many amazing places on our trip! We also met a lot of interesting people along the way. Look at the map below. Use your finger to trace all the places we have been.

What states have fewer people than Alaska? *See page 9 for the answer.*

What is the tallest mountain in North America? *Page 14 has the answer.*

What is the largest glacier in North America? *See page 17 for the answer.*

What is Alaska's major road? *Page 18 has the answer.*

What happened at Attu Battlefield? *Look on page 22 for the answer.*

What city is the state capital? *Turn to page 28 for the answer.*

How big was Jack Tragis's halibut? *Look on page 30 and find out!*

How many miles does the Iditarod cover? *Turn to page 34 for the answer.*

ARCTIC OCEAN

BEAUFORT SEA

Barrow

Prudhoe Bay

RUSSIA

Nome

ALASKA

Fairbanks

CANADA

Alaska Range

BERING SEA

Anchorage

Valdez

Liarsville

Skagway

Juneau

OIL

Alaska Peninsula

GULF OF ALASKA

Sitka

Unalaska

Ketchikan

PACIFIC OCEAN

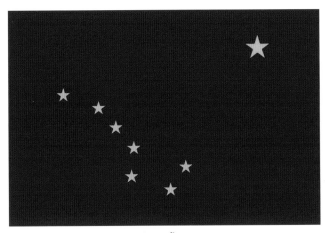

State flag

State seal

STATE SYMBOLS

State bird: Willow ptarmigan

State fish: King salmon

State flower: Alpine forget-me-not

State fossil: Woolly mammoth

State gem: Jade

State insect: Four-spotted skimmer dragonfly

State land mammal: Moose

State marine mammal: Bowhead whale

State mineral: Gold

State sport: Dog mushing

State tree: Sitka spruce

STATE SONG

"ALASKA'S FLAG"

Words by Marie Drake, music by Elinor Dusenbury

Eight stars of gold on a field of blue—
Alaska's flag. May it mean to you
The blue of the sea, the evening sky,
The mountain lakes, and the flow'rs nearby;
The gold of the early sourdough's dreams,
The precious gold of the hills and streams;
The brilliant stars in the northern sky,
The Bear—the Dipper—and, shining high,
The great North Star with its steady light,
O'er land and sea a beacon bright.
Alaska's flag to Alaskans dear,
The simple flag of a last frontier.

That was a great trip! We have traveled all over Alaska! There are a few places that we didn't have time for, though. Next time, we plan to visit the Valley of Ten Thousand Smokes. It's located along the Alaska Peninsula. There are 15 active volcanoes there!

FAMOUS PEOPLE

Baranov, Aleksandr (1746–1819), Russian fur trader, politician

Beckerman, Marty (1983–), author and journalist

Bering, Vitus (1681–1741), explorer

Boozer, Carlos (1981–), basketball player

Brooks, Alfred Hulse (1871–1924), geologist

Call, Marian (1982–), singer

Egan, William (1914–1984), first elected governor

Eielson, Carl (1897–1929), pioneer pilot

Fletcher, Rosey (1975–), snowboarder

Gaines, Ruben (1912–1994), poet

George, Jean Craighead (1919–2012), children's author

Gomez, Scott (1979–), hockey player

Jackson, Sheldon (1834–1909), missionary and educator

Jewel (1974–), singer, songwriter

London, Jack (1876–1916), author

Mala, Ray (1906–1952), actor

Muir, John (1838–1914), naturalist

Riddles, Libby (1956–), champion musher

Rock, Howard (1911–1976), editor and publisher, activist against nuclear testing

Thomas, Khleo (1989–), actor

Tosi, Mao (1976–), football player

WORDS TO KNOW

antlers (ANT-lurz) bony structures like horns on the heads of deer and related animals

dorms (DORMZ) short for dormitories; buildings where a lot of people sleep

folly (FOL-ee) something foolish

frontier (fruhn-TIHR) an unexplored region

industry (IN-duh-stree) a type of business

legends (LEJ-uhndz) imaginary tales that people tell to explain their world

peninsula (puh-NIN-suh-luh) a piece of land almost completely surrounded by water

rendezvous (RON-day-voo) French word for a meeting

thunderbird (THUHN-dur-burd) to Alaska Natives, a huge bird with magical powers

traditions (truh-DISH-uhnz) customs and ways of life handed down from generation to generation

tundra (TUHN-druh) soil that's frozen beneath the surface all year round

TO LEARN MORE

IN THE LIBRARY

Bjorklund, Ruth, William McGeveran, and Laura Sullivan. *Alaska*. New York, NY: Marshall Cavendish Benchmark, 2016.

Daly, Ruth. *Denali*. New York, NY: AV2 by Weigl, 2013.

Funk, Joe. *Mush! Sled Dogs of the Iditarod*. New York, NY: Scholastic, 2013.

Miller, Debbie S. *Survival at 40 Below*. New York, NY: Walker & Company, 2010.

Oachs, Emily Rose. *Alaska: The Last Frontier*. Minneapolis, MN: Bellwether, 2014.

ON THE WEB

Visit our Web site for links about Alaska:

childsworld.com/links

Note to Parents, Teachers, and Librarians: We routinely verify our Web links to make sure they are safe and active sites. So encourage your readers to check them out!

PLACES TO VISIT OR CONTACT
Alaska Travel Industry Association
alaskatia.org
610 E. 5th Avenue, Ste. 200
Anchorage, AK 99501
907/929-2842
For more information about traveling in Alaska

Anchorage Museum
anchoragemuseum.org
625 C. Street
Anchorage, AK 99501
907/929-9200
For more information about the history of Alaska

Alaska covers 665,384 square miles (1,723,337 sq km). It's the largest state in size.

INDEX

Bye, Land of the Midnight Sun. We had a great time. We'll come back soon!